I Killed

•

I Bled

Blaise Cendrars

I Killed / I Bled

Translated and with an Introduction
by Rainer J. Hanshe

ERIS

ERIS

265 Riverside Dr
New York, NY 10025

Contents

Introduction

Rainer J. Hanshe

The dawning of a new century on the rise: construction of the Eiffel Tower, symbol of industrial and artistic progress and icon of the Enlightenment, concludes in 1889, the centenary of the French Revolution and founding of the First Republic. Not long thereafter, Freud and Jung will expand the fields of the mind and construct equally monumental conceptual structures, mapping the unconscious and the shadow, presaging the mapping by physicists of dark energy and dark matter in the late twentieth century. In 1905, Einstein will publish his theory of special relativity, and in 1915 his theory of general relativity, exploding notions of space and time, consequently provoking a revolution as monumental if not greater than the Copernican. It is also the epoch of cinema, its birth oft considered to be 28 December 1895, the day the first film was screened at the Lumière brothers' Cinématographe. Conversely, the terrors of WWI would bring to bear against the promise of a new century, the potential that is of an ever-more pacific and refined civilization, its first forbidding foil.

In the midst of these events, the Swiss-French writer Blaise Cendrars, who was born the year construction on the Eiffel Tower began, establishes himself as one of the most intrepid and iconoclastic figures of the twentieth century. Nomadic writer par excellence, Cendrars began his writing life as a poet and would have his hand in almost every art, and pen almost every kind of text, from poems to stories and novels to reportage, radio plays, ballet texts, and film scripts. He also worked as a translator, anthologist (of African myths, legends, poems, and modern writing), and with Cocteau and Paul Laffitte, founded Les Éditions de La Sirène, co-editing and overseeing projects such as a monumental edition of Casanova's *Mémoires*, reprints of Villon, Nerval, Baudelaire, Lautréamont, and Apollinaire, not to speak of, as he would have us believe, tracts, anthologies, mystical writings, Alexandrian and Byzantine novels, painters' sketchbooks, and more. Cendrars's activities were not, however, restricted to the ateliers and editing rooms; he was active on battlefields, too.

In 1914, to defend his adopted country, Cendrars would join the Foreign Legion and fight in WWI, which interrupted his writing life due not only to the consumption of his time but, more significantly, to the loss of a limb. He fought on the front line at the Somme, where he was stationed from mid-December 1914 until February of 1915. Seven months later, on 28 September 1915, while fighting in the battle of Ferme Navarin in the Marne Valley, Cendrars would lose the lower half of his right arm, his writing hand.

These war experiences feature in several of his books, including *La main coupée* (*The Severed Hand*)

and what follows hereafter in English translation, "J'ai tué" ("I Killed"). He does not speak of the maiming in "J'ai tué"; that trauma is what opens "J'ai saigné" ("I Bled"), the later autobiographical counterpart to *J'ai tué*, which is more sanguine and melancholic, more anguished, an explicit account of the injury. Significantly, the wound figures in *La main coupée*, where, twenty-eight years later, Cendrars transforms it, referring to his lost hand as a red lily, its fingers anxiously digging into a floor to take root: "une grande fleur épanouie, un lys rouge, un bras humain tout ruisselant de sang, un bras droit sectionné au-dessus du coude et dont la main encore vivante fouissait le sol des doigts comme pour y prendre racine et dont la tige sanglante se balançait doucement avant de tenir son équilibre."[1] The stigma of the wound clearly remained over time, but if Cendrars's physical, if not psychic, equilibrium was under threat, mytho-poetic energies seem to have brought him a sense of balance. Although he started writing *La main coupée* as early as 1918, it would not be published until 1946, making "J'ai tué" the first publication about his time as a soldier.[2]

Maimed but not broken, Cendrars would eventually regain his desire, as well as the physical ability, to write; perhaps, as he explains in a poem written prior to *La main coupée*, it emboldened him to uphold Orion as his polestar, as well as his lost hand itself, a dead limb transformed into a living constellation:

ORION

This is my star
It has the form of a hand
It's my hand rising to heaven
During all of the war I saw Orion through a crenel
When the Zeppelins came to bomb Paris they
     always came from Orion
Today I have it above my head
The great mast pierces the palm of that hand
     that must hurt
Like my severed hand hurts pierced as it is by a
     continual sting[3]

In 1916, while struggling with the psychic lacerations of the horrors of the war, as well as the trauma of losing his writing hand, Cendrars trained himself not only to type one-handed, but also to write with his left hand.[4] If at least one poem, "La Guerre au Luxembourg,"[5] and one short prose text, "Profond aujourd'hui" (1917), predate "J'ai tué," the latter is one of his earliest post-WWI texts, one of the first he writes with his left hand.[6] As a brief account of the war, "J'ai tué" could be characterized as reportage, but how closely it hews to fact and personal experience is indeterminable. On the original title page of the book, Cendrars himself refers to his text simply as "prose."

Richard Sieburth calls "J'ai tué" a "laconic, shell-shocked first-person report from the trenches," yet, although laconic, it is hardly the report of a shell-shocked person. It is too alert, too incandescent, a stroboscopic prose poem whose cadence and beat replicate the swift, sharp, severe cadence and beat of war as well as its vile odors and vulgar realities. The text is hyper-lucid, suffused with energy, force, and dynamism, as muscular, if not as violent, as war itself, but perceived from the vantage point of Cendrars's Brahmin-like consciousness. The noises of combat, its demonic precision, and how its infernal machinery functions with a terrible, regimented logic—like the ordered days of Sade's *120 Days of Sodom*—make Cendrars think of mathematics and the music of the spheres. Equally so, the respiration of the world itself evokes for him Baudelaire's poetics.

These are not the reflections of a soldier partisan to violence, and this consciousness, a grander, all-seeing cosmic perspective that abjures nationalistic and militaristic rhetoric, informs "J'ai tué." Set as it was in red ink, it is explicitly a text of blood, one born not only of lacerations, injuries, and wounds, but murder.

In relation to the effects "J'ai tué" conveys, whether or not Cendrars himself actually murdered a German soldier is immaterial, for its principal concern is in depicting how even a poet can be dehumanized to such a degree, mutated, that is, into an ape-like marionette of pure matter, that he will commit murder. This mechanization and fragmentation is also evident in Léger's fractured Cubist drawings, where not only space and time collapse upon one another, but the human body itself is split and violated, if not crushed, by the overfull world around it. Not whole, not distinct, but uniform, as if cut in slices by the rigors of war, though still alive. In one of the drawings there is even an image of a dangling arm free-floating in space, adjacent to a bandaged soldier with what seems to resemble a tear beneath his eye, a probable reference to Cendrars's own wound, if not to any maimed or disfigured soldier.

All that the Eiffel Tower symbolizes is then questioned in "J'ai tué" as a force that has likewise contributed to horror, to an irrepressible power that can possess even the most refined—the poet—and turn him into a murderous fiend, yet, as Cendrars intimates, the entire earth is complicit. The pronoun "on" (we) is generally used throughout the text, Cendrars only switching to "Je" (I) in key moments, one an instance of individuality, of the reverie the poet has of Baudelaire, another when the ghastly machinery of war has taken possession of the poet and extinguished his individuality. If this is an individual, it is one denuded of self, an "I" of the herd, only a number, a functionary. This brute reduction is explicitly signaled at the end of "J'ai tué," when the enemy is seen not as a human, but as an ape. Invoking the *lex talionis* and the Old Testament, the poet himself is also no longer human, but an avenging savage whose sense of reason has gone amok. If one of ours is killed, one of yours must be killed as well.

Is this pure inevitability, an inescapable probability programmed by the Commander-in-Chief's prayer calculus of violence?

As Cendrars says in *La main coupée*, "war is not a pretty sight and what you see when you take an active part in it, when you are just a simple man lost in the ranks, a service number among millions, is altogether stupid and seems to obey no overall plan but chance. To the expression 'march or die' could be added the axiom 'go wherever I push you'! And that was exactly how it was: we went, we pushed, we fell, we died, we got up, we marched and we started all over again."

This clearly evokes Abel Gance's antiwar film *J'accuse*, which was shot in 1918 and first released in 1919, just one year after the completion of Cendrars's text, which he wrote while on set working as Gance's assistant. Cendrars is featured in its final haunting scene, wherein soldiers are depicted rising from their graves, returning to question the living about why they were killed, and what, if anything, they died for. Gance also used other veterans who had been disfigured in the war, many of whom resemble the malformed, monstrous subjects of some of Otto Dix's more gruesome paintings and etchings. This cavalcade of actual mutilated figures renders palpable the gruesome effects of war, the resurrected soldiers a terrible *j'accuse* that sends the rest of society fleeing in horror.

The creation of Cendrars's "J'ai tué" and Gance's *J'accuse* are then intertwined, each perhaps informing the other, both antipathetic visions of war, something undeniably horrific to Cendrars, a man who even carried trunks of books with him on his journeys into the Brazilian jungles. When the Gestapo ransacked his house during WWII, destroying his entire library, Cendrars said it brought about the temporary extinction of his personality.[7] Afterwards, he did not write for many years, language having gone silent in him.

Even if an amorphous, ephemeral strength, language remains a strength, though one that does not necessarily enable us to survive terrors. Although it is a dwelling place, if it endowed the Hungarian poet and genocide victim Miklós Radnóti with sustaining energy in his final days, it did not save him from execution, nor did the strength of language sustain Nerval, nor Celan, nor Gherasim Luca. There are many others, too, for whom language is an unreachable power, one both feared and considered threatening, as can be the books we make with it. But if language is lost, when the barbarians threaten to undermine culture by destroying it, whether through burning books, pulverizing statues and other unique artifacts, or through murdering satirists and thereby silencing a critical and creative power, then humanity itself is under threat of extinction, just as Cendrars personally felt temporarily extinct through the destruction of his library. Language is a subtle, lasting strength out of which a civilization can be built, but if lost, the power to create a civilization is also lost. Without books, without the singularity of language, there is our definite erasure. The ape is not far off.

BLAI
CEND

I Killed

1914 / 1918

They come. From every horizon. Day and night. 1,000 trains disgorge men and material. In the evening, we cross a deserted city. In this city, there's a large hotel: modern, fancy, square. It is the G.H.Q. Cars with flags, packing crates, a swinging oriental chair. Very distinguished adolescents, in impeccable chauffeur's clothes, talk and smoke. A yellow novel on the sidewalk, a spittoon, a bottle of cologne. Behind the hotel, there's a small villa hidden behind the trees. You can barely see the facade. A white shape. The road passes in front of the gate, turns, and runs along the wall of the estate. We're suddenly marching on a thick bed of straw that absorbs the sluggish noise of thousands and thousands of oncoming boots. All you hear is the rustle of arms rhythmically swinging, the clink of a bayonet, a bracelet, or the flat thud of a canteen. The breathing of thousands of men. Muffled pulsation. Involuntarily, everyone sits up and looks at the house, the very common little house. A light filters between disjointed shutters, and in this light an amorphous shadow comes and goes. It's HIM. Have pity on the Grand Chief Officer's insomnias, for he brandishes the table of logarithms like a prayer machine. A calculation of the probabilities knocks him cold. Silence. Rain. At the end of the wall, the straw stops. Soon we'll be paddling together in the great tide again. This is the dark night. Marching songs begin again.

Catherine has pig feet
Ugly ankles
Knock-knees
A musty crack
Rotten breasts

Here are the historic roads stretching up to the front.

Ours are the broads
With hair on their asses
We'll watch 'em again
When the troops (repeat)
We'll watch 'em again
When the troops'll return

....

Soldier, grab your gear
Now you see him, now you don't
My old buddies!
Another Arab gets fucked in the ass
In the officer's trench

....

Grumpy Father
Pull down your pants
Look, here's the sausage (three times)
For Alsatians, Swiss, and Lorrains

....

Bang, bang the Arbi
The jackals are over there

....

It was a spring evening
In the far-south a marching troop

....

Then the Bat d'Af' passes
Breaks out and out again
Save for the Tonkinese
Within three months they pull out

....

Trucks rumble on. Left, right, everything moves awkwardly, heavily. Everything advances in jolts, in jerks, in the same direction. Columns, masses give way. Everything trembles. It smells of a horse's burning ass, Motosacoche, phenol, and anise.[1] The air is so heavy, the night so suffocating, the fields so putrid it's like swallowing rubber. Father Pinard's stinking breath poisons nature.[2] Long live Aramon, which burns in the belly like a vermilion medal![3] Suddenly a plane takes off in an explosion of backfire. Clouds engulf it. The moon rolls behind. And the poplars of the national highway spin like the spokes of a vertiginous wheel. The hills tumble. The night cedes to this pressure. The veil is torn. Everything breaks, cracks, booms out at once. General commotion. A thousand blasts. Infernos, fires, explosions. An avalanche of cannons. The thunder roll. Barrages. The firing pin. In light of the looming departure, oblique, ambiguous men, an index finger on a signboard, a mad horse. The batting of an eyelid. The flash of magnesium. A snapshot. Everything disappears. We saw the phosphorescent sea of the trenches, and the black holes. We pile into the parallel trench, crazy, hollow, haggard, drenched, exhausted and flushed out. Long hours of waiting. We shiver under the shells. Long hours of rain. A little cold. A little tobacco. Finally dawn creeps in. Devastated countryside. Frozen grass. Dead soil. Sickly pebbles. Cruciform barbed wire. The eternal waiting. We're under the arc of the shells. We hear the big honeys enter the station. There are locomotives in the air, invisible trains, crashing, smashing up. Including the double blow of Rimailhos.[4] The toiling of the 240. The great fart of the long 120. The roaring spin of the 155. The crazy meow of the 75. An archway opens over our heads. Sounds drop out in male and female pairs. Gnashing. Hissing. Ululating. Neighing. This thicket spits, trumpets, screams, cries and laments. Steel chimeras and rutting mastodons. Apocalyptic mouth, open pocket from which inarticulate words plunge, huge as drunken whales. They interlock, form sentences, take on signification, redouble in intensity. It's precise. A particular ternary rhythm can be discerned, a proper cadence, like a human accent. Over time, this terrifying din is really no more noticeable than the noise of a fountain. One thinks of a jet of water, a cosmic jet of water, for it is regular, orderly, continuous, mathematic. The music of the spheres. The breathing of the world. I clearly see the plain breasts of a woman gently stirring with emotion. Rising and falling. So round. Powerful. I think of Baudelaire's "The Giantess." A silver whistle. The colonel leaps forward with open arms. It's H-hour. We march to the attack smoking cigarettes. Immediately the German machine guns go rat-a-tat-tat. Coffee grinders rotate. Bullets crackle. Marching forward we raise the left shoulder, shoulder blade twisted to the face, every bone disarticulated to make ourselves into shields. Our heads burnt with fevers and anxiety in full flush. We were jittery. But march on all the same, calm and well aligned. There is no chief officer any more. Instinctively we follow the one who always showed the most composure, often a lowly private. No more bluff. There are even a few bawlers who are killed shouting: "Vive la France!" or: "For my wife!" Generally, it's the most taciturn who take command and lead, followed by a few hysterics. This group stimulates the others. The braggart vanishes. The ass brays. The chicken hides. The weak fall to their knees. The thief abandons you. Some even pick your pockets. The cowardly turtles sneak into the trenches. Others play dead. And a whole gang of poor devils are slaughtered without knowing how or why. And they die! Now the grenades explode in the deep water. We're surrounded by flames and smoke. And a senseless fear knocks us into the German trench. After a vague clamor, we recognize each other. We organize the conquered position. The guns go off alone. We're all suddenly there, among the dead and wounded. Without respite. "Forward! Forward!" We don't know where the order comes from. And we start by abandoning the plunder. Now we march in the tall grass. We see demolished cannons, upturned landmines, fields scattered with shells. Machine guns fire at you from behind. There are Germans everywhere. We have to cross the barrage of gunfire. The great black Austrians crush and boil an entire section. Limbs fly in the air. A gob of blood hits me in the face. We hear heart-rending cries. We jump into abandoned trenches. We see heaps of corpses, ignoble as the sacks of rag pickers; shell holes filled, to the brim, like garbage cans; terrines filled with nameless things, juices, meats, clothing and stacks of shit. Then, in corners, behind bushes, in a sunken road, we see the humiliated corpses, frozen like mummies, making a little Pompeii. Planes fly so low you have to duck. There's a village to seize down there. A big take. Reinforcements arrive. Bombardments resume. Winged torpedoes, trench mortars. After half an hour, we rush forward. Twenty-six of us make the position. The prestigious setting of crumbling houses and gutted barricades. I should clean it. I have the honor of being issued a switchblade. About ten of 'em are dealt out and several large melinite bombs. Here I have the flick-knife in hand.[5] The whole immense war machine comes down to this. Women worked to death in factories. A population of laborers toiling excessively in mines. The striving of scientists, inventors. Every marvelous human activity is paying its tribute. The wealth of a century of intensive work. The experience of many civilizations. The entire surface of the earth is working only for me. The minerals come from Chile, the conserves from Australia, the leathers from Africa. America sends us machine tools, China sends workmanship. The rolling horse was born in the pampas of Argentina. I smoke Arabian tobacco. I have Batavian chocolate in my rucksack. The hands of men and women have made all that I carry with me. All races, all climates, all beliefs have collaborated. The oldest traditions and the most modern techniques. The bowels and morals of the globe are upsurged; still uncharted regions have been exploited and harmless beings have learned an inexorable trade. Entire countries were transformed in a single day. Water, air, fire, electricity, radiography, acoustics, ballistics, mathematics, metallurgy, fashion, arts, superstitions, the light bulb, travel, the table, the family, and the history of the universe is the uniform I wear. Steamers crossing the oceans. Submarines diving. Trains running. Lines of trucks reverberate. Factories explode. In big cities crowds rush to the movies and fight for the papers. Deep in the countryside farmers sow and reap. Souls pray. Surgeons operate. Financiers get richer. Godmothers write letters. A thousand million people have dedicated to me for a day all their activities, their strength, their talent, their science, their intelligence, their habits, their feelings, their hearts. And here today I have the blade in my hand. The flick-knife of Bonnot. "Long

live humanity!" I feel cold truth cut by a sharp blade.
I'm right. My young athletic past will suffice. Here I
am, nerves tense, muscles bandaged, ready to leap
into reality. I braved the torpedo, the cannon, mines,
fire, gas, machine guns, the whole anonymous,
demoniac, systematic, blind machinery. I'll brave
man. My fellow. An ape. Eye for eye, tooth for tooth.
Between us now. At fists, at knives. Merciless. I jump
on my antagonist. I deal him a terrible blow. The
head is almost peeled off. I killed the Kraut. I was
livelier and faster than him. More direct. I struck
first. I have a sense of reality, me, the poet. I acted. I
killed. Like one who wants to live.

Nice
3 February 1918

I Bled

1938

In memory of Miss Y. Soubeiran of Bovril (New Zealand)

I

Sister Philomena

Champagne 1915.

It was the day after the great offensive failed.

Forty-eight hours after my amputation, a new attack was being prepared in the area, the commissariat needed my bed and my bloody shirt. And it was then that I found myself stark naked on a stretcher in the courtyard of the wire factory where my operation had been carried out, awaiting the arrival of a convoy of Ford health workers who were to evacuate us—hundreds more wounded were groaning in every corner of this huge factory yard littered with pieces of machinery and dismantled boilers—from surgical station 55 toward the rear.

The sky was black. It was raining nonstop.

It could have been 9, 10 at night. It was the 1st or 2nd of October.

The shelling and musketry from the front came very close to us, and behind me, a shot from the 75 fired point blank at the enemy planes whose buzzing razed the factory roofs and made us even more afraid than the heavy explosions which, to the left and to the right, would crush what was left standing of the ruins of Somme-Py.

We saw men falling or lying down, jumping to the ground. Others stepped over my stretcher splattering me with mud. Still others trotted in horror, running to bolt between the iron scrap heaps that, in collapsing, bury them. Everywhere there was nothing but leaks, cries, screaming, moaning, groans, and my severed arm hurt me so bad that I bit my tongue to keep from screaming, and frequently I shivered because I was cold, under the rain, like this, entirely naked, stretched on my narrow gurney, immobile, ankylosed, annoyed that I couldn't move on my own, like someone who had given birth to a newborn child, embarrassed by the enormous bandage, big as an infant, pressed close to my flank, this foreign thing that I couldn't move without stirring a world of pain, or take it in my good hand without seeing that big white pad itself becoming soaked with red, I felt an atrocious burning and realized that my life was escaping me, going away, drop by drop, without my being able to do anything, because you cannot stop your heart, and my heart, which was beating regularly, with each stroke I felt it sent forth a rush of blood, as if I had seen it, squirting from the end of my severed arm—and these morally and physically unbearable pulsations allowed me to measure time, of which, when I was alone amidst the furious melee of this horrible night, I recorded every detail, itself flowing inexorably, that is, in its true nature, of seconds, of fractions of a second, of eternity.

Two, three hours passed.

Between two planes, between two stampedes, between the sequences of the 75 that fired at the mouth, what do you want, between the collapse of neighboring buildings, porters, nurses, bustled the great wounded who had to be evacuated at all costs from the old territory, circulated, like porters on a press day sticking release labels to parcels, evacuation cards, and it's then that a sergeant, panic-stricken and teeming with fear, attached my amputee record to my ankle, without a word, without a glance at the naked man who turned blue with cold under the rain. And what's funnier is that this sergeant wasn't the misleading type and that it was my personal record that he had given to me, as it later turned out.

The cars arrived after midnight. They entered full throttle into the courtyard, were loaded at full speed, started in reverse, turned on two wheels before the gate, recovered and raced in fourth gear, in the shrapnel-filled night, weaving between demolished houses to catch the road, the wide demolished road that led to the rear.

Ambulances entered in twos and threes, because the convoy had been bombarded on the outward journey and the drivers were eager to leave again, afraid of being caught in return fire because, according to their words, they wanted to clear out before an ammunition convoy that they had passed by on the road would arrive in Somme-Py, and they didn't want to be pinned down, come under fire by this reinforcement that would surely unleash ammunition on the unfortunate village. All their words were alarming, and giving a hand to the team of porters, the drivers threw into their cars the operated patients of post 55, most of whom, in ordinary times, would have been deemed untransportable.

Finally, one of the little Fords stopped before me. It picked up a poor guy who was to my right; then another who was a bit further away; a third was fetched from I don't know where behind me, and then, it was my turn. But the driver, a tall, bearded man, exclaimed: "Ah, no, wait! We've seen everything! I'll get a blanket…" And the good man went away and came back with a rag and threw it at me, saying: "There, old man. Now, let's get the hell out. It's disgusting, but you'll be warm…" And we embarked, me, fourth in the van, made to slide head first into its mouth as into an oven, and he buckled a tarp over me. And the ambulance drove off with a jolt, which made the four poor bleeding devils scream in pain, bandaged and bruised as we were.

I remember that it was the man who was lying down, next to me, to my left, who began the music.

The Ford scuttling ahead so fast that it could make the congested road sweat and slip through places riddled with shell holes.

The little car that carried us swayed, lurched, skidded on the shoulders where it was playing leapfrog with the piles of stones, where then, it jerked, ricocheted, colliding from one hole into another, and when the engine was racing we were shaken as in the devil's cup-and-ball game.

Like a hysteric cramped on his mattress or like a mystic in a trance whose disoriented spirit flees into the beyond and whose stigmatized remains, abandoned on my bed, arch and begin to gravitate, I stand firm on my stretcher in order to make my body hover through all these bumps and jolts, the least of which precipitated me into a beyond of acute suffering that was less than human and from where I fell, plunging into the bottom of my wound like on a narcotic, my mind into an abyss.

—Oh!... Ow!... we groaned. And sometimes a cry, a long howl of pain tore us apart, and I would've been embarrassed to say which of us four, and if it wasn't me, had uttered this howl, this cry which sounded like an animal and which made me ashamed, while the ambulance sped as fast as it could...

—Mommy!... Mommy!... yelled the man lying above me. O mommy!...

And that's when the music began in that infernal ride and until we stopped at Châlons-sur-Marne.

—Mommy! Mommy!... grumbled the guy lying above me. O mommy!...

—*Halt Schnurre, Sauhund!*... insulted my neighbor below, while his neighbor from above lisped:

—*You can't shut your trap can you, huh? The lady your mom isn't there, stupid so, she's not goin' to come, you louse, see here. It isn't 'easonable at all, kid, no, louse, not for a little sou! Me, the medic told me I'd have both legs cut and me, I didn't yell about that, louse! You can't shut up, hey, say then mistuh? You, what a big baby...*

But as the wounded man above moaned in a more
and more acute voice, asking for his mama in a groan
that stretched, crescendo and decrescendo, and the
German, my neighbor, swore at him to keep quiet,
the black, suddenly a raging madman, started rais-
ing hell up there, banging on the tarp and
bellowing:

*—Drivuh, drivuh! Beat it, beat it! Just get me down.
There's a dirty Kraut in there! Long live F'ance!*

The fever was rising and I was about to faint—
from horror, pain, dizziness, exhaustion—when
suddenly the car stopped and a soft female voice says
to us from outside:

—Give me your files quickly, kids. You're in luck.
Just now there's a nice train to Biarritz. Come on,
hurry up!...

We were in a suburb of Châlons. And as they
unbuckled the tarp and their hands fiddled about us,
overseeing our evacuation forms, stamping, checking,
registering them, I saw an arm hold a bottle of cognac
out to me, and I heard another female voice say:

— Here, drink; it will do you good, little one...!

I grabbed the bottle eagerly. But already the car
was off again. "Bon voyage! Bon voyage!" shouted
voices. I emptied the bottle in one gulp and... I
believe I fell asleep.

When I regained consciousness my stretcher had
been placed in the courtyard of the station. Blue
lights were reflected in the puddles and the clock
struck three in the morning. I heard a wailing loco-
motive and an interminable train passing on the
rails. I thought they would soon come to get me.
Lying level with the pavement and almost under the

chassis of a car, I was more or less sheltered from the rain and not worried about my fate since the motor was idling and sent its hot breath into my face, spoke to me of its misfiring. Only my severed arm hurt me.

The train that rolled into the station pulled away. The rain was still falling... The gutters disgorging. The motor went silent... and I made a new plunge into sleep or unconsciousness, which a searing pain drew me back from. It was the ambulance driver who, all on his own to get me back into his car, seized my stretcher as best he could, that is to say by crushing my arm, and swung me unceremoniously on board.

The man was furious:

—Oh, hell! The bastards, the loafers! No one to lend a hand, he grumbled. They only think of cozying up to the fire, the cows. But me, I'd also like to go hit the sack... You can't imagine that, all the same, it's fun at this hour to roam around the city yourself, he added, seeing that I had opened my eyes. Eh, well, my buddy, if you think it's funny! And then, you made sacred music all along the way! Ah, no, I'm sick of it, you know. It's damn ugly, their fucking war. I'm tired, and I'll desert if it lasts a long time...

Then he relents:

—I hurt you, huh, poor old man? Don't blame me, but those hospital porter bastards, they make me shit. We gotta rely on ourselves, the rest of us. They don't give a damn. I've already made two trips this night. The Krauts have us played, and with dragging around poor guys like you, what do you want, me, it drives me crazy, I can't get used to it. Me, I'm a mechanic; I wasn't in the slaughterhouse. You think there's nothing to catch jaundice from, to see all these cushy bastards by the station who make farces with the Ladies of France and their swollen major! And the top brass, eh, let's talk, my colonel! To make some zealous, he did it, the bastard. I'd shove a bayonet deep in his stomach when I stretch him out saying that the wounds that we give him are nothing at all. Then with you, he didn't want you to embark on the train to Biarritz. He said that you had a temperature and that you were drunk, and he turned you around!

—So, where're you taking me? I asked the driver who was getting ready to get his motor running again.

—Well, I'll take you to Sainte Croix, to the bishopric, it's a good hospital. And then, it's a stone's throw from my garage. I'm beat, you understand. I know someone who will suffer.

—And the bishopric, is it far?

—Don't worry. A quarter of an hour. And you can pamper yourself. It's a good hosto. It's rich, St. Croix, and it's full of ass. As for the grubmaker, she's famous. My word, you're lucky to run into me and I stick by that. This is the right place I tell you and you can believe me. Another would have led you straight to the military hospital. But with the priests you'll be well cared for. So don't worry. You're in luck.

—And the others? They aren't coming, the others, I'm all alone?

—Damn, you're curious, you. What's with you? So, you gotta know everything? And what were you doing in civilian life, some chump, taking care of others? No, you're stupid, you! Don't you want a cig sometimes?...

And turning to hand me a lit cigarette, which he planted in my beak, the cockroach was working this chatter, and the war made him cynical, if not loony, he told me, settling in his seat and leaning on me:

—Well, since you wanna know everything, I'll give it to you. The great jaws of the Senegalese and the total-Fritzs, they're in the train, and they give fuck-all about you, you can believe me, at this hour they drive toward Biarritz. As for the little one who was blubbering and bugging us about his mama, right? eh, well, he snuffed it, so there! You've seen nothing then. When we wanted to get off at the station, he spilled all his blood through the mouth. Good god, you're all red. Haven't you noticed? And my blanket, it's ruined and I'll have to snag another. Oh, there, there, what a job, we're never finished!…

And the driver turned his back to me, made his gears creak, and sped away through the winding streets of Châlons, taking turns real close, rattling, zigzagging on the accursed cobblestone in the roundabout of the old city.

I don't know how long this infernal truck of the Red Cross took to bring me to the bishopric, and I can't say when, nor how this race ended, because during the drive, I had to die and rise again a few dozen times. But when I came back to life for the last time, I was surprised to find myself completely naked on my stretcher, except that it was being put in the middle of a gigantic hall, all in ornamental woodwork.

A majestic oak staircase, which gave me vertigo, rising, rising, four, five, six floors, the gleaming and well polished wood floors, and I was lying upside down, facing the roof, lost, up there, in the black, and I pondered the massive joists.

Not a sound. Not a crack. I was awed. The silence was absolute.

This pompous architecture, this grandeur, austerity, nobility, the proportions of everything, the dimensions of this monumental staircase, the armorial panels, the calm, the peace, everything was from another age, from another century, from another era, everything seemed hostile, and as nothing moved, I began to be horribly afraid, afraid of being forgotten in this defunct decor and of the sole light bulb going out in the magnificent chandelier that filled the dark, vast stairwell from above to below.

I had to fidget on my stretcher, gesticulating; gesticulating not only with this left arm, which I didn't yet know how to use, but also brandish this right hand, this hand that I had just lost, which had just been stolen from me in Champagne, which I had left behind me in the mass grave of Somme-Py, and whose astonishing presence was itself revealed, manifested, felt in the exorbitant pains that manifested from my stump, grew, ramified, tugging at me in all directions, made me writhe as if I had been consumed in an inner blaze, became widespread, but remained nevertheless very precise all while multiplying as if I had been cut off, not an arm on a circular saw, as with Buddha, a range of arms constantly reborn, a bewildering sensation that made me leave myself, which troubled my most basic reflexes, disoriented me, unbalanced me and made me lose even the exact notion of my bodily dimension.[1]

The fever, the exhaustion, the bottle of cognac that I had absorbed in one gulp, the bumps in the road, the horror, the fright of transshipment, the stench or the belch of chloroform or of camphor oil, the hunger, the fatigue, the sensation of vertigo and of falling, the shelling, the wounded, the hardships, the cannonade of the attack, the bombs, the explosions, those returning from the battle, the firing of the German machine guns that massacred us in the barbed wire, the man that I had nailed with a blow of a knife, my carried off arm, the screams of buddies, this desire to get away and live, the exaltation, the others, the dead and the thousands, the thousands more wounded, the surgeons among whom I myself was discussed, the blood that spurt, the cold that overcame me and the sudden fear, the intense fright of being snuffed out there, on my stretcher, the jitters about falling asleep, to faint and pass out without realizing it, the terror of being forgotten, all this made me delirious, and I had to scream, to call for help, to shout with all my strength in the rich and beautiful sleeping ecclesiastical dwelling, or at least I imagined that. But, perhaps, when I imagined myself screaming with all my might, I could hardly breathe or moan low or groan, barely able to breathe, because, in reality, I was exhausted. In any event, I have the memory of having lived a fierce, long, and insidious struggle, but as brutal as possible, so as not to lose consciousness completely, not to surrender, to slip into a coma.

I remember at one point a bell ringing in my ears, or so I thought I remembered that when he went away, before taking his blanket from me, the driver who abandoned me in this sumptuous hall had spoken of a bell to be rung to make the world come running; in short, I remember that at one point the bell or the notion of a bell troubled my brains and I made desperate efforts to get up and pull the rope of the bell that was dangling somewhere in the corner of the deserted hall, and this bell, probably ghostly, I heard it, repeatedly, ringing at full speed in my head and, every time, my despair to see this bell, which hurt me, which woke no one, was infinite.

So there I was, watching for the angel of death who was about to swoop down onto me to take me into his soft and warm wings, and asphyxiating my head under his armpit, and I had already sensed his presence reflected in the decor that became blurry when I perceived, suddenly, a rustling of robes, the twitch of a rosary and dainty medals and, like a mouse nibbling in silence, a furtive sliding down the stairs. And my attention was drawn by a hand that was placed there, up there, high up, on the dark railing, and the white hand descended slowly toward me, from the sixth to the fifth, from the fourth to the third, from the second to the first floor by following the noble spiral of the banister, and at the first landing I saw grow gradually as she descended the last steps, a woman dressed in black and wearing the flickering wings of a cornet, Sister Philomena, who hesitated the more she approached me, and then she froze on the penultimate step, long enough to sigh, "Oh, my sweet Jesus, a naked man!" to bring her hands to her heart and to fall in one piece across my stretcher.

Poor Sister Philomena, so sweet, so appropriate, so stubborn in the prayers that she had subsequently recited each night in my room of the severely wounded as one prays to exorcise, I believe that she could never conquer the fear that my vision had caused her the night of my arrival at the hospital. Retrospectively, she must've been ashamed of her weakness.

—It's not the blood with which you were coated, from head to toe, that had scared me, my poor little one, but your surrender. I did not see the man, but the mortal... the mortal sinner...

—You're right, my sister, because I have killed. Today, we are millions of men who, weapons in hand...

Yet Sister Philomena had not come to pray in my room but more to chat with me. She had her truth. As soon as I opened my mouth, she withdrew to kneel down, enveloping me in signs of the cross.

II

The Death of the Little Shepherd

If, in the night, we were watched over by the sisters, during the day it was the registered nurses of the Association of the Women of France who took care of us.

The upper floor of the bishopric had been converted into a blood lazaret to receive 150 to 200 seriously wounded, but the day after that unfortunate offensive of Champagne we were a good 500.[2]

The lead nurse, Mrs. Adrienne, who was responsible for these pitiful victims mass-produced by automatic weapons and war surgery, was a woman with a big heart.

I stayed nearly a month in the Châlons-sur-Marne Hospital and I had time to consider that the dedication of our nurse was immeasurable.

Mrs. Adrienne P... was engaged in her terrible and often very repugnant medical task with such enthusiasm, such tact, and so much delicacy in her skill and thoroughness in the care that she lavished us with, an insistence made of authority and persuasive sweetness—not to mention the gifts, treats, the nice touches with which she graced her dear wounded and which very seriously had to empty her purse— that at first sight each of us, with great difficulty escaping from the slaughter and still muddy from the trenches, had the impression, then were quickly convinced, that we were the favorites of this woman jealous of her kids, so everyone felt spoiled, pampered, cosseted, loved, and morally supported and comforted by this volunteer nurse whose active charity, despite her other duties, went so far as to serve as secretary for corresponding with families—and God knows if the letters of the blasted WWI soldiers in full youth were harsh confessions, accusations charged with ruthless and terrible curses to the addressed parents, teachers, or to the homeland or beloved woman, regrets, considerations about life, despair, overwhelming desires, childish and disturbing confessions, or lies due to pride that the lead nurse perceived each day, which wasn't to facilitate the correspondence of this voluntary, lucid, attentive, and courageous witness, but sensitive and overworked, which was to transmit, alas! often after the first news of a serious injury, the announcement of a fatal outcome and as voices of condolence, the last will, that is to say nine times out of ten the curse of a soldier who had been sacrificed, but who had defended himself, at the hour of his vehement death, from having wanted to be a hero.

In the bishopric, the wounded from upstairs had such devotion for their nurse that I saw trepanned patients smile, madmen, anxious people calm down or act carefree, feverish people keep quiet, restless people control themselves, one-legged people running too early on their crutches to please Mrs. Adrienne, and to reward her, I even saw the dying get themselves off their asses, show off, salute, make graces, affirm that now they were out of the situation, and die with ease. But I also saw Adrienne P...., after her exhausting day's work, pass white nights at the bedside of one of those battered wretches that were lowered to her every day directly from the front and whose soiled stretcher was deposited in a small padded room, because their condition was desperate and because their distracted screams were more vile than their shredded flesh; I saw our nurse implore surgeons to attempt the impossible, struggling all night, syringe in hand, dosing out morphine to relieve the pain of a martyr soldier and burst into tears when the man's heart gave way and that this stranger, registered but anonymous, passed from life to death.

Her gift of herself was complete, without any restriction, without ulterior motive, absolute. Mrs. Adrienne P... attended each of her wounded in the operating room, she personally and tirelessly remade the most complicated and painful dressings, and she didn't trust anyone else with the funereal chore of bathing till death, she would keep watch of the body in the chapel, she accompanied the remains to the cemetery, no longer as an award-winning nurse, but as supreme tribute from a woman, in deep mourning, and, every time, she came back from a funeral doleful, stumbling, collapsing in her sails, letting herself go like a mother who had lost her only son— and then, if her service allowed it, she took refuge in my room and spoke of her deep sorrow. Those days, as we had very quickly become good, very good friends, this valiant woman, whom the whole hospital admired, admitted to me the deadly lassitude, the neurasthenia, the disgust that secretly overcame her, and this ardent soul was not ashamed to truss herself up and to have in my presence two, three shots of caffeine to pick herself up, to stay abreast of the task she had imposed on herself and not to allow herself to lose her strength, not to let her nerves betray her.

For, is it not that I am a woman, daughter, granddaughter, great-granddaughter of French officers, and I have no children, she told me one day. My husband had the misfortune of serving in the offices in Paris. I felt that it was my duty to come to the line of fire. And what wouldn't one do to save honor and France...wouldn't you, Mr. Cendrars?

If I don't absolutely despise women it's because I knew this one and met two, three other nurses of the same grit during the war, who all knew how to pay with their own lives.

Like a miser her treasure, Mrs. Adrienne P... jealously guarded certain wounded whom she let no one approach and whom she fought for by disputing with the too standardized and too enterprising supervision of military doctors and surgeons.

These selected wounded were installed in a suite of good small rooms, narrow as cells, and Mrs. Adrienne barely kept her privileged ones under lock.

I was not one of them, although Adrienne pampered me in a special way, bringing me, every morning, luxury cigarettes (Muratti-Lauriston, with gold tips), at noon, some flowers (she had to bring them from Paris), during the day, books (works by Gringore, St. Amant, Scarron), coming to keep me company when she had some leisure time, chatting with me, lingering, taking pleasure in my recounting my adventurous life in China or America, forgetting her weariness, but not allowing anyone else to undo and redo my dressing;—and what was my simple, healthy amputation compared to the multiple wounds, the complicated fractures, the unprecedented trepanations, the insidious respiratory diseases, the blindness, the mental or functional disorders of the gassed, the broken jaws, the traumatized, the paralyzed, the dazed, the anxious, those blind only by vigils of strength, perseverance, stubbornness, daring, inventive genius, divination in little cares at all times, but also heart, prayers, appeals, patience, love, tenderness, maternal protection, did this woman rescue little by little from death or from despair?

One day, Mrs. Adrienne came to find me:—I'm not mistaken. Cendrars, coming for you? I have here a poor little shepherd from Landes who is suffering like a martyr. I'll have you carried into his room. You will have your books and all your other stuff, but I absolutely count on you to distract him. I know it won't be fun for you, because the poor guy is an orphan, he doesn't talk much, and you must attend at least once a day to his dressing, which is a terrible thing, but I don't know anyone else who can cheer him up. Maintain him, tell him stories, it will do him good. Would you like? Pardon me, won't you, Cendrars?

This poor little shepherd from Landes was a worthless little soldier, a Class 15 rookie that a shell had riddled with shrapnel before they had appointed him his foxhole,[2] even before he had time to put his sack on the ground and turn around a bit to see what the famous front line trenches were whose country he was talking so much of.

Very brown hair and eyebrows, narrow forehead, dark eyes, dark complexion, his face gaunt, his cheeks hollow. Lying upside down, the face of this adolescent disappeared almost entirely in the pillows. His features were distorted by suffering, and when the pain made him shriek, I saw his lips tighten, discovered his young wolf teeth, a vein that swelled at the root of the nose blocking his forehead, pinching his nostrils. He closed his eyes and the sweat of anxiety moistened his neck and temples.

Indeed, he was a taciturn boy and our beds almost touched in the narrow little room, if I may call the bulky frame in which he didn't rest a bed, but the unfortunate one hung by straps, hoops, belts, and a rack and pinion system, like an ox at work, his buttocks in the air and for forty-nine days already!

He had received 72 bits of shrapnel in the lower back, which made 72 deep, penetrating wounds, and of all sizes, including a large round hole that pierced through and through laterally and that was infected with fecal matter. They had removed umpteen kilos of scrap metal from his buttocks, shapeless pieces, pieces like saw teeth, splinters like packets of fine needles, and also, extraordinary thing, a hundred franc piece (that's what made the big round hole in him that was infected), a silver coin that the poor little shepherd of Landes said he had not had in his pocket when he was hit, being an orphan, with no one, not even a wartime godmother and never having dreamed one day of being able to have that kind of money.

Operated on a dozen times already and still having other surgeries in view because of this infection that had a tendency to spread, and new shrapnel that traveled into his flesh and had to constantly be extracted, it was crazy what this little soldier had to endure in twenty-four hours, although copiously drugged since, hitting a temperature in the evening, his nights were spent in agitation and delirium; but the most excruciating moment of the day was for him the hour of being bandaged, which weighed on his conscience, and which he dreaded—and when that hour approached and we heard medics and nurses advancing in the hallway, he began to scream in terror before what awaited him.

I cannot describe this session that I was obliged to attend every day since Mrs. Adrienne had me share the torture chamber of the innocent supplicant, but, in retrospect, I still shudder when I think of it. Suffice it to say that it was necessary to extract 72 bits from his 72 penetrating wounds, curette them one after another, washing everything in bleach, unclipping, searching thoroughly, cleaning, irrigating with saline, putting new bits in place, then tackling the transverse hole made by the franc piece, draining out, probing, giving injections, trimming, cutting, pinching, puncturing, tearing out, fraying, pouring tincture of iodine down the hole, putting the drain in place, dressing that poor whining thing, stirring, shaking, flipping, changing his position, restrapping him, bathing him, remaking the bed, and it took three clock hours every afternoon, it was that complicated. The surgeon was leaving when he had done his work with his claws, his curette and forceps, the doctor was anxious to disappear as soon as he had given injections and shots, prescribed drugs and medications, diet, and it is on Mrs. P..., on this poor friend Adrienne as on a hangman, that fell the responsibility to go without trembling to the end of this cruel treatment. I admit she was doing it with dexterity, even failing to faint when this masterpiece of its kind was finally over.

—You understand why I am disgusted, Cendrars, she said to me, sitting on my bed. I can't take it anymore. Yet I am very proud of this little one! It's me who got him there and got him this treatment. They wanted to butcher him, and me, I wanted to save him. I know it is painful and it will be a long process. But, my good friend, if you knew what that poor little guy has already been through. He was doomed. Ten, twenty times, the doctors wanted to give up, saying there was nothing more to do, the infection was winning. But I held on and, now, I assure you, he will already be much, much better, and the surgeon himself claims that his case is not hopeless...

A smell of rot, of camphor, of phenol, of Peruvian balsam, feces reigned in the superheated alcove. The little shepherd of Landes, freshly bandaged, lay like a bitching lamb. Mrs. Adrienne P... laid her head on my shoulder and I patted her hands with my good hand.

—I admire you and I pity you, I told her.

But Mrs. Adrienne was already fleeing because other wounded were demanding her care.

My severed arm was hurting me.

—Dirty war! I said aloud.

Despite the individual dramas that played out in each bed of this extremely urgent lazaretto, the games of life and death which are the usual humdrum business of a hospital, time passed relatively easily at the bishopric of Châlons-sur-Marne because man is accustomed to everything, and even, outrageous thing to say, even to not being respected in his physical integrity.

The thought was abominable to me, and so as not to feel physically diminished by the amputation of my right arm, after several days of hospitalization and as soon as I was able to sit up in my bed, every morning, at dawn, I boxed a quarter of an hour into my pillow. My arm was bleeding profusely, but I paid it no mind, overcoming pain to endure repeated and faster and faster blows with my stump.

If on the nineteenth day the surgeon attributed to this repeated exercise the record healing of my arm, a healing that was so surprising that he subsequently recommended to all amputees to engage in the same kind of exercise, I attributed, me, other virtues to boxing, and more particularly the entirely mental one of restoring to myself the notion, if not of completeness, at least of my body balance.

This is how, after boxing, I started to juggle in my bed, with oranges, with small objects, learning to use my left hand, with strength, and with dexterity, but also using my right arm as a shortcut to return a ball or to hold a dish, glasses, a cup, in equilibrium. (And it's always for the same reason, not to feel myself physically diminished, once returned to civilian life, that I started to practice all violent sports and games of skill, such as football, swimming, mountaineering, horseback riding, tennis, basketball or billiards, pétanque, pistol shooting, fencing, croquet, darts; thanks to which, today, I pilot both my race car and I am typing or making shorthand with my left hand, which gives me joy.)

Joy, I didn't ask for so much then, in my hospital bed, when I gave myself up to my first exercises, simply contenting myself to take pleasure, childish pleasure, in seeing that I was not too clumsy.

Besides, the little shepherd that Mrs. Adrienne had told me to distract was much more amused by my juggling and balancing exercises and my feats, as well as by my stories.

Poor kid! It's that little shepherd from Landes who made me realize that if the human mind could conceive of infinity, then it's because the pain of the human body is also infinite and that horror itself is unlimited and boundless.

III

Poor tyke!

One afternoon, around four o'clock, we had to complete the painful dressing of the little shepherd and my bedmate lay exhausted, stupefied by a massive dose of pantopon,[4] and, me, I was quietly reading, when the rumor spread in the rooms and hallways that a famous doctor, a master of the Academy, director of I don't know what Paris hospital, and who, if I remember correctly, was to be called something like Professor Dufossé or Desfossés, in short, a top dog, who had the rank of general, was going to give an inspection of the bishopric and, immediately, at the announcement of this visit, St. Croix was turned upside down.

We only heard running footsteps in the hallways, loud voices, orders, the noises of chairs, of beds jostled in the next room. Nurses came, went, changed the linen, bringing fresh towels, pillowcases, patting the sheets, pulling the blankets, arranging bottles and trays, carrying out latrine buckets and everything else lying around, pieces of clothing, crutches, treats, hobbies, card games, books, magazines, newspapers, handicraft manuals, faded flowers, old cigar boxes that contained memories of the hairy war: uniform buttons, epaulette brackets, German chargers, aluminum rings, lighters made of cartridges, love letters, photos, etc., and, on their heels, coming, going, auxiliary cleaning women who came to give a clean slate, dusting, polishing, ventilating the rooms, redoing the folds of the curtains, emptying the ashtrays and the gazunders. Convalescents slipped furtively from a room into an alcove, very excited by the news that they were peddling, announcing the general evacuation of the hospital, the move to hotels on the Côte d'Azur or the immediate reformation implemented with all these poor devils, the sensational news that the top dog doctor would confirm forthwith. But if some of these talkers very much rejoiced as children in their prompt demobilization and their speedy return to their homes, which they believed in good faith, others, more clever or more suspicious, went to bed, absorbing rotgut one after another, alcohol, drugs to give themselves fever, scratched themselves, ready to aggravate wounds and injuries, not feeling sorry for anybody and not to leave the good life in the hospital, but because they knew from experience that the coming of a great leader never bodes well for a soldier, and these clever ones kept quiet, ready to believe that they were at the point of death and regretting not having had all four limbs amputated.

Amidst all the bustle appeared Mrs. Adrienne, whom they had fetched from her home in the city.

—I am very annoyed, Cendrars, she said to me as she entered the room and glanced anxiously at the little drowsy shepherd. Hush, he's sleeping! I just learned that we have the order to undo all the bandages. The Inspector wants to see our wounded one by one. He's a general. He will arrive at any moment. And I cannot inflict the poor little one's punishment twice in one day! He wouldn't resist. What should I do?

—My God, Mrs. P... turn off the lights and lock our room with the key.

—It's impossible.

—So, start the tour at the other end of the hospital and take this illustrious professor everywhere, to the kitchen, the laundry, the cellar. Show him the pharmacy, the autoclave, the cabinets, hide nothing from him, stroll through all the nooks and crannies, and maybe this general will want to go and, if it's late, we'll be forgotten, us two. It's already past 4:00; he won't sleep here, will he? In an hour or two he'll have had enough. Drag things out.

—You're probably right. But you don't know the health service inspectors. They will search everywhere, of course, but it's especially for our little wounded one that I'm worried. Provided that nothing bad happens! I'm not calm. Imagine that he lingers around and he asks us how, why, and this, and that, and he wants to lay hands...

—But no, but no, dear lady. You're nervous. You exaggerate. What can the general do to this poor kid? In the state he's in, he won't even look at him. Besides, you'll be present, and if he wants to touch him, the surgeon and you, you only have to tell him that this is impossible, that we cannot make two dressings in one day, this is too terrible. Look, show him his temperature chart; he had a big flare-up again today. This general is still a doctor, damn it, he'll understand.

—You think?

—But of course! Listen, dear friend. Don't touch this little one. But you'll undo my dressing to show my arm is healed, and when I hear him coming, that great bogeyman of a general, I'll post myself on the threshold of the door to prevent him from entering and say to him that I was better cared for than at home.

—I absolutely forbid you to get up, Cendrars!

—And why not! Get me any old clothes, since I arrived totally naked and I didn't even have a uniform, and you'll see! You know, Adrienne, the surgeon cannot believe that my arm is already healed. He claims that I beat a record! Eh, well, today, I want to impress him, and I'll keep standing, I swear, to receive him, him and his general, and the President of the Republic, if he comes!...

I hadn't meant to brag, but I overestimated my strength. The head nurse had barely come out when, wanting to get up alone, I went and stretched myself full length on the polished floor, falling with all my weight on my severed arm, which hurt me worse than the day when I was wounded on the battlefield by a machine gun bullet. Nevertheless, when Adrienne returned a few moments later, with a large dressing gown she had gone to fetch for me, she found me standing, clinging to the bars of my bed, and, at 5:00, I had taken a few steps in the room and Mrs. P..., if not reassured about the fate of her little shepherd, was at least satisfied with me, could go to meet the general whose arrival was announced by a bell.

At 6:00, I began to drag my firm foot.

At 7:00, I was straddling a chair, experiencing a slight seasickness because everything was beginning to sway around me.

At 8:00, I was lying on my bed, but ready to get up at the first alarm when we were informed that dinner would be served.

It was already 4:00 when the life of the house was suspended for the visit of this general whose inspection, which was endless, disturbed the order and the smooth pace of the services of the hospital.

Between 8:00 and 9:00, the disorder was at its height. The temperature had not yet been taken and 500 wounded in treatment had a cold supper, served in haste by the scullery maids. I learned from those maids that, on arrival, a stormy session was held in the office of the superintendent and the general had yelled at the surgeons, doctors, and nurses. Everyone was on edge.

At the time of the relief, the nuns told me that the famous practitioner of Paris was shut up in the operating room and for two or three hours he sawed arms and limbs to lecture the staff of the bishopric. Everyone was shocked, and it seems that wounded were moving a lot and generally temperatures were rising.

A little later, Sister Philomena, on lookout at the top of the stairs, came to tell me that "they" were all feasting, the General Intendant, the doctors, the lay nurses, "they" do not seem to get bored because "they" talked and laughed loudly in the dining room on the ground floor, the doors were pushed against. And Sister Philomena seemed indignant.

It was about 10:30, 10:45, when my roommate, who until then had remained asleep, opened his eyes and asked:

 —Hey, old man, what's going on?...
 —What?
 —They're making a big stink!...
 —But no.
 —But if...

—I assure you not. You were out of it.

—…So why didn't they come to take my temperature this evening?…

—You were sleeping.

—Then…, why weren't we made to eat?…

—You were sleeping. I told them not to bother you once you were snoozing without a hassle.

—…Hey, man, I had a nasty dream…

—Ah!

—Yes… I dreamed that, that… Say, do you not think that I'm worse… I dreamed that I was going to die, and now I'm sure I'll be taken out…

—You're talking bullshit.

—You think?… So, tell see, why is it that Adrienne didn't come tonight, as usual… I'm not more sick, huh?…

—Adrienne? But don't worry, she'll come. You see, I'm waiting. I got myself dressed. We're going to play a good joke on her. You're going to laugh.

My neighbor turned around painfully. I stood up in my vast dressing gown draped like the statue of Balzac. The little one looked at me.

—It's funny, that's funny… he stammered. Like you are great… But, tell me, what's up?…

—What?

—I don't understand… Why are you dressed?… Are you leaving me, huh?…

And after a long silence, the poor sufferer asked, even more worried:

—…But tell me, what time is it… You hear them… Looks like they're coming!…

Indeed, we heard a commotion in the corridor. Immediately, the small Landes boy screamed in terror:

—Ah!... Oh!... No!... I don't want, I don't want to!... Adrienne!... I beg you... This is not the time!... Ah!... Oh!...

He was completely crazed.

—What's going on, what's happening there? shouted a loud voice.

A group invades the room. 11:00 struck.

—So, you're the one screaming like that? said a fat man in a white coat, knocking on the door jamb.

Mrs. Adrienne, our surgeon, our physicians, our nurses, other members of the day and night staff, including military nurses pushing the bandage carts, escorted this big jovial man, whose braided kepi, planted askew across his skull, discovered the congested face, dented forehead, venous temples, punk mustache, bad teeth and small laughing but acute eyes of the most intense blue.

—My general, I said to him, look, I'm healed! My arm is healed. I move it. You know, I juggle and I fight with it. And I haven't been here three weeks. I was injured on September 29th. It's a record!

And I began to juggle with three tennis balls that I had prepared.

The inspector burst out laughing—But that's fine, my little one, go to bed. But that other one, the hanging man, what's with him? he asked Mrs. Adrienne, who had rushed to protect her little martyr.

The head nurse proceeded to provide detailed explanations about the injury, the wounds, extracting many shards, the history of the franc piece, giving details of the following treatment, appropriate care, and the delicacy of fighting with the infection, the suffering endured by the patient who was getting

better and who the surgeon claimed was now out of
the woods. The general listened with great attention,
while the little shepherd bawled like a donkey: "Ah…
Oh…," articulating nothing else.

The room was full of people.

I sat up on my bed.

—Give him the temperature chart, I whispered to
Sister Philomena who was standing before me.

—Undo his bandages, ordered the professor when
consulting the documents. I want to see him.

—No!… no!… screamed the kid.

—Don't agitate yourself, Mrs. Adrienne said to the
little struggling child, though she diligently undid
the bandages. It will be nothing. It's for your own
good, you'll see.

—Hurry up! said the general, as he and the
surgeon donned their rubber gloves, the dressing
trolley advanced, and the one who was operating the
bed rack presented the wounded in a good position
and the curious circle tightened so as to lose sight of
nothing of what the great and famous practitioner of
Paris was going to say or do.

Adrienne gave me a desperate look.

The Inspector General was equipped with a clamp
and a lancet.

He brutally ripped the bits, one after the other,
bent over the holes in the buttocks, sniffed them
closely, probing each wound, then, without being
bothered by the inhuman cries of the little peasant,
he removed the drain from the large lateral hole,
nudged him, sat up and said, making a grimace:

—I congratulate you, Madam, and I admire your
courage. But this method will not get you anywhere.

It's a work of patience, a real puzzle, but you're wasting your time. All these honeycombs are all foci of infection, hence these temperature surges and irregular jumps of the graph. What ground you believe to have gained one day is lost the next, because that ground is mined. What is it about? We're on a battlefield. The ground is mined. We cannot wait, remain at the mercy of the enemy. We must fight against time, outrun the enemy, so we don't beat around the bush but practice contra-sapping to get a result, brutally and by surprise. Give me my scalpel. Na, thanks. I'm not going to take care of the surface funnels, as deep as they are. The danger isn't there. But I have to detect the main focus, the center of the infection, the mine blast that could explode in our face, play tricks on us from one moment to the next. I say, therefore, that we need to bring all these funnels together, trace a network of trenches that all lead to the main trench, which will subsequently allow a deep irrigation, and flush out the enemy wherever it hides. No traffic jams, that's not it; in a field so distraught, we would lose. But a wide access road that leads directly to the central fireplace. Attention, one-way traffic, with only one entrance, only one exit. We make one incision, another, still another, very deep, and we're in the sap as in a central sewer, under the Place de l'Opéra. The entire surface drained, we'll take care that the center, which, although cleared in depth, remains within reach. I put a clip up high, I add flaps, I...

Having joined action to word, the eminent professor of the Faculty who harangued the gallery as if he

were in his class, before his audience of students,
carved into the heart, brought together the 72
wounds, unleashed them in a single, broad, deep
move, and he fought his way so beautifully that after
a fifty-minute demonstration, the soldier was dead.
But the little shepherd of Landes hadn't been yelling
for a while now.

IV

A Word from Life

At the end of my stay at the hospital in Châlons-sur-Marne, I had the opportunity to attend, in another small bedroom in the attic of the bishopric where Adrienne had once again put me, always under the pretext that I was in good spirits, a true, genuine resurrection.

The injured man I was keeping company at this time was a huge company sergeant, so heavy, so tall, and of such size that they had to, if not reinforce, at least add an extension to his bed to support his feet, which exceeded it.

This colossus had been trepanned once and then again, after which, the first time, he had remained paralyzed on the right side and, after the second, he had lost the power of speech. He was a big, docile, greedy, and clumsy infant, who spilled his soup on the sheets and who flew into ridiculous rages when someone wanted to touch the big top gunner's coat spread over his bed, in the folds of which shone a brand new Legion of Honor cross that this baby-adult with smoldering eyes and numb fingers caressed continuously, even in his sleep, like a baby's rattle.

And it was quite pathetic to see Adrienne, who had to sit at his bedside several times a day, rehabilitate this man who, muscular, strong, and well-proportioned too, to teach him again the use of his limbs, to give him a glass ball in the palm of his hand, saying clearly and emphatically the words: ball-round-cold, watching in his intelligent eyes if those words

42

aroused some notion in his conscience or, like a child, present a colored alphabet and try to make him read, to make him say with her the following letters, syllables with his fingers: DA-DA = DADA, TO-TO = TOTO, HA-HA = HA HA, etc.

—Did you notice his eyes, Cendrars, when a spark ignited in them? Adrienne said to me after each session. He's made great progress since you've been here, you know. I'm sure he now understands everything said to him. Soon, he will speak.

And the nurse left full of faith, attending to her other work, going back two, three hours later to give the man-baby another laugh and start teaching him everything from the beginning with a wonderful, angelic, and inexhaustible and radiant patience.

This gunner was a very handsome man with very regular features of great distinction, to which the dressing that crowned his head, far from fading or darkening, added indescribable brilliance, what nobility. Rendered frail by his injury he looked like a turbaned Byzantine prince and even his clumsiness, which was more like languor than paralysis, did not completely deprive him of his natural state, some innate elegance that makes me hesitant to qualify the awkward poses of this bedridden man—and small disasters resulted from it for him because his brain was deflowered by a foreign body and cut by the scalpel—of royal blunders. His eyes were more vivid, more mobile, more meaningful and, indeed, they expressed many things.

It was astounding, and it was a constantly renewed pleasure, and often an enjoyment when I succeeded, only to look into his expressive eyes to decipher, guess, understand in a flash what his look meant.

How can one express so many things through the eyes? I do not mean moral or abstract things, because my questioning did not go so far, but the obscure needs of organic functions, and of the quasi-vegetative life that normally verges just below consciousness, are repressed or too indecent to mention and which the eye, the gaze of this silent trepane, made me somehow understand when he was hungry, thirsty, or needed to do his business.

Mrs. Adrienne was right, there was a great advance because, since I was sharing his room, this half-paralyzed casualty followed me with his eyes when I moved around him, juggling, boxing, giving myself to all sorts of relaxation and balance exercises and continually addressing him so as to get his attention, no longer was he done under, no longer did he soil himself, except at night.

One night—it was around dawn—I awoke with a start.

My neighbor was sitting on his bed, comforter, sheets, blanket pulled down.

I don't know how he had taken the position, but the cripple was standing on his bed.

His eyes looked like two very bright stars and he made desperate efforts, jaw contracted, hanging open, the throat agitated, mouth wide open to try to say something—a word that was on the tongue, at the edge of his lips, and which he could not expel.

Immediately, I rang, I called, I ran into the hallway, I alerted everyone, and in no time Sister Philomena, and other sisters, the stretcher-bearer and the night nurse, the night-watch doctor of the surgical unit surrounded the bed of the handsome artilleryman who, more and more tense, chest protruding, muscles bulging, flexing his whole being so much with his will, was grand, stood there, mouth open, the tragic mask, his eyes wide with envy, without managing to belch.

Two, three hours passed and everyone anxiously wondered what would happen, when about seven in the morning, someone had hurriedly gone to wake Mrs. Adrienne, and when seeing his nurse enter the room, the triumphant voice, the rolling eyes, transported and fainting, our good childlike giant cooed: C-A-C-A = CACA! before relaxing. And while everyone was busy around him, Mrs. P..., filled with joy, jumped on my neck:

—This is the best day of my life. Blaise! she spoke. Now, he is saved. Thanks, thanks.

And, me, I was very embarrassed, not knowing what to do, not only because Sister Philomena looked at us and because I knew I did not deserve the compliments of this teacher-woman with whom I had the first few hours of peace and joy since the war, but because for the first time in my life I found myself hugging with one arm a woman...

So, not to feel this embarrassment, and at the amazement of all, I made with the head nurse three, four swaying waltzes, singing:

I have danced not just once with her...

and whispering in her ear:

—Adrienne, thanks, thanks from all of us. We love you...everyone!

Notes

Introduction

1 Blaise Cendrars, *La main coupée* (Paris: Editions Flammarion, 1975) 118.
2 The original publication featured five wood engravings by Fernand Léger, a close friend of Cendrars. The text was printed in red ink, two of the engravings were printed in blue and two in red, and the cover was blue and yellow. The book was 18 cm x 18.5 cm and enclosed in a blue Morocco clamshell case and limited to 353 copies.
3 "Orion," *Le Formose* (1924). The small star just above Cendrars's right shoulder in Modigliani's *Portrait de Blaise Cendrars* (1916–18) is a subtle reference to this.
4 Cendrars had at least two different mechanical limbs but abandoned use of them. Albert t'Serstevens recollects the final rejection of the device: "Maurice Barrès gave him a marvelous orthopedic device, an arm made of ash wood and aluminum which, with the slightest pressure, clenched the fingers on their metallic hinges. For a while, Cendrars enjoyed using the limb. He just abandoned it in a station; when he was going on a trip, he deposited it at the left luggage

office, thus lightening his load." See *L'homme que fut Blaise Cendrars* (1972) 414–15.

5 This features six drawings by Moise Kisling. It was published in 1916 by Daniel Niestlé, who had also volunteered to fight in the Foreign Legion and was a friend of both Cendrars and Kisling, another veteran. The book is dedicated to three of their dead comrades. Upon publication, the cover was censored. In one signed copy of the poem Cendrars ironically refers to it as "this little book about the first games of a new civilization."

6 At the end of his life, Cendrars would suffer from hemiplegia, which paralyzed much of the left half of his body, once again making writing a challenging, if not difficult task. He died in Paris on 21 January 1961 and was first buried in the Cimetière des Batignolles. Thirty-three years later, his remains would be transferred to Tremblay-sur-Mauldre.

7 Cendrars was wanted by the Gestapo due to his involvement with the British Expeditionary Force as a war correspondent for *Paris-Soir*. These articles were collected in *Chez l'armée anglaise* (Paris: Corrêa, 1940) but, prior to publication, the Gestapo confiscated the book and destroyed most copies of it. Cendrars recounts this story in *L'homme foudroyé*, the first volume of his autobiographical saga.

I Killed

1 Motosacoche is a Swiss motorcycle manufacturer, founded in Geneva in 1899 by Henri and Armand Dufaux. At the first Bol d'or in Paris (1922), which was held in the Forêt de Saint-Germain, the winning rider covered a distance of more than 750 miles on a 500cc Motosacoche.

2 Pinard was a type of red wine (of the Burgundy variety) rationed to French troops during WWI. The soldiers affectionately dubbed it Father Pinard and

the term moved beyond their lexicon and became popular after the war.

3 A variety of red wine grape that is blue-black in color and which hails from the Languedoc-Roussillon region of southern France. It is also referred to as Ugni Noir (Provence), Rabalairé, Pisse-vin, Gros Bouteillan & other names.

4 A reference to the 155mm Rimailho Howitzer, used by France during WWI, which was designed by Capt. Emile Rimailho, a French artillery officer. Its name is also similar to the archaic French verb *rimailler*, which means to write bad poetry, an echo surely not lost on Cendrars, and clearly intended.

5 Cendrars uses the word *"eustache"* here, Parisian slang for a switchblade invented by the infamous criminal and anarchist Jules Bonnot. The Bonnot Gang (1911–1912) used cars and repeating rifles prior to their being available to the police. The socio-political orientation of the gang was informed by the ideas of Bakunin, Proudhon, Stirner, Ravachol, and Nietzsche. Cf. Richard Parry, *The Bonnot Gang* (1987).

I Bled

1 This description is reminiscent of the passage in *Le Lotissement du ciel* (*Sky: Memoirs*) where Cendrars describes the sensation of his phantom limb: "the mind strays, trying to follow, to situate, to identify, to localize the existence of a severed hand, which makes itself painfully felt; not at the end of the stump or in the radial axis or at the center of consciousness, but as an aura, somewhere outside of the body, a hand, hands which multiply and grow and fan out, the fingers virtually crushed, the nerves ultra-sensitive, leaving an imprint on the mind of the image of the dancing Shiva revolving under a circular blade, severing off each arm, one by one..." (1949) 66–67.

2 A medical facility specializing in the care of contagious patients. From the Italian *lazzaretto*, a leper hospital or place of quarantine. One was established in America (Tinicum Township, PA) in 1799 in reaction to a yellow fever epidemic. It functioned for nearly 100 years, closing in 1895.

3 Cendrars uses the word "cagna" here, French military slang for dugout (it also means female dog, canine, bitch), which comes from the Vietnamese *cái nhà*.

4 Pantopon: an opiate derivative used to treat diarrhea and taken orally (in the form of a drip or a pill). Side effects include drowsiness, fainting, and lightheadedness. Taking excess pantopon can cause seizures, irregular breathing, and severe weakness.

GPSR Authorized Representative: Easy Access System Europe, Mustamäe tee
50, 10621 Tallinn, Estonia, gpsr.requests@easproject.com